The Lotus Life

DR. ANKITA GUPTA

NewDelhi • London

BLUEROSE PUBLISHERS
India | U.K.

Copyright © Dr. Ankita Gupta 2024

All rights reserved by author. No part of this publication may be reproduced, stored in a retrieval system or transmitted in any form or by any means, electronic, mechanical, photocopying, recording or otherwise, without the prior permission of the author. Although every precaution has been taken to verify the accuracy of the information contained herein, the publisher assumes no responsibility for any errors or omissions. No liability is assumed for damages that may result from the use of information contained within.

BlueRose Publishers takes no responsibility for any damages, losses, or liabilities that may arise from the use or misuse of the information, products, or services provided in this publication.

For permissions requests or inquiries regarding this publication, please contact:

BLUEROSE PUBLISHERS
www.BlueRoseONE.com
info@bluerosepublishers.com
+91 8882 898 898
+4407342408967

ISBN: 978-93-5989-018-0

Cover design: Shivam
Typesetting: Namrata Saini

First Edition: February 2024

Dedication

To myself, Dr. Ankita Gupta, for standing tall amidst the storm.

In the wake of my mother's cancer battle, I found strength not just for myself, but for my young son and my family. Navigating through the societal expectations of a woman particularly in developing countries and patriarchal societies, balancing the demands of a professional career, and coping with immense personal turmoil, I've journeyed through a path that tested every fiber of my being.

This book is a tribute to that journey – to the resilience in adversity, to the courage in despair, and to the unwavering spirit that carried us through.

Acknowledgements

This book, a reflection of my journey and insights, would not have been possible without the unwavering support and love of several remarkable individuals in my life.

First and foremost, I extend my deepest gratitude to my parents. Their constant support and the invaluable gift of education they have provided has been the bedrock of my life. They have been my guiding stars, illuminating the path of knowledge, wisdom, and compassion.

To my mentors, guides, and teachers, I owe a debt of gratitude for instilling in me a robust value system and for shaping my thoughts and convictions. Their teachings have been instrumental in molding a spirit of understanding and motivation in me. To my most beloved Son- his presence in my life has been a source of endless inspiration, encouraging me to pursue my passion for writing with zeal and dedication. His wisdom belies his years, and his influence is a golden thread woven through the tapestry of my work.

I am also immensely grateful to my friends and colleagues, with whom I share the daily ebb and flow of life. Their companionship and unwavering faith has been a source of strength and perspective, helping me navigate through life's myriad challenges.

My heart goes out to all those who are often tagged as the Misfits, the Black Sheeps and the Eccentrics who have always inspired me with their spirit of resilience against these societal frictions.

Finally, I acknowledge with profound respect those who have consciously or out of sheet ignorance put me through dark times. It is through these challenges that I have discovered my own resilience and strength. These experiences have been crucial in my personal growth and evolution, teaching me invaluable lessons about life, love, and the indomitable human spirit.

To all of you, I extend my heartfelt thanks. Your influence has been a vital part of my journey, and this book is a testament to the richness you have brought to my life.

Preface

"The strongest oak of the forest is not the one that is protected from the storm and hidden from the sun. It's the one that stands in the open where it is compelled to struggle for its existence against the winds and rains and the scorching sun."
- Napoleon Hill

In the heart of every struggle lies a story of resilience, much like the lotus that blooms untarnished in muddy waters. "The Lotus Life" is my ode to this resilience, a poetic journey through the trials and triumphs that shape our existence.

This book is born from the interplay of shadow and light, exploring themes that resonate with the rhythm of life. The verses are symbolic to a journey meandering through the deepest recesses of human heart, mind and soul - experiencing tribulations on its way and turning them into a beautiful rhythmic melody called Life.

From the intricate dynamics of married life in the poems like 'Silent', 'Murderer' , 'Once More' to the societal challenges faced by women talked about in the poems like 'Sold', 'Shameless' , 'Perfect' , these poems delve into the depths of hardship and the soaring heights of the human spirit.

There are echoes of courage, perseverance, and an unwavering belief in the possibility of transformation and the significance of second chances in life in verses like 'Firefly', 'Rainbow' and ' Golden Hour'.

Amidst these reflections on struggle and strength, there are also whispers of idyllic love and companionship in the poems titled 'Paradise' and 'Euphoria'. These poems serve as beacons, illuminating the path through dark times, guiding towards a haven of inspiration and solace.

Then there are poems like 'Destination', 'Extraordinary', 'Fear', 'Escape' and 'Green' that speak of life's profound philosophies, urging the reader to think and embrace an out of box ideology as not just a virtue but a way of being.

This collection is also an intimate exploration of psychological resilience. It seeks to unravel the complexities of mental abuse and the faces of abusers, offering insights into confronting these realities and evolving beyond them. The verses like 'Smiling Assassins' and "Facade' , 'Intimidating' , 'Naked' and 'Content' are not just words; they are therapeutic revelations, intended to guide, heal, and empower.

My muse and motivation in penning down these verses is my mother, a warrior in her own right. Her battle against cancer has been nothing short of heroic. She is the embodiment of the *Lotus* in my life – rising, blooming, and thriving against all odds. Her strength and grace under pressure have been my guiding light, inspiring me to find beauty and wisdom in the most challenging situations.

"The Lotus Life" is more than a collection of poems; it is a journey of transmutation, a testament to the human spirit's capacity to grow and flourish in adversity. It is my hope that these verses resonate with you, offering a mirror to your own struggles and a window into the infinite possibilities that await ahead!

Foreword

Tanvir Ahmed
Assistant Professor
Department of English
Baba Ghulam Shah Badshah University Rajouri, J&K

In an era where resilience has become a necessity, "The Lotus Life" by Dr. Ankita Gupta emerges as a beacon of hope and inspiration. It is my distinct honor to introduce this poignant collection of poems that delve deep into the human spirit's capacity for strength and transformation.

Dr. Gupta's work is a rare blend of personal introspection and universal truth. Her verses, rich with emotion and insight, offer a window into the trials and triumphs that define the human experience. From the intricate challenges of married life to the broader societal issues faced by women, her poems traverse a landscape filled with adversity, yet always find a path leading towards hope and enlightenment.

What makes "The Lotus Life" particularly compelling is its foundation in real-life resilience. Inspired by her mother's courageous battle against cancer, Dr. Gupta's writing resonates with authenticity and power. It is a testament to the enduring strength of the human will and the transformative power of adversity.

This collection is not just a series of poems; it is a journey. A journey through the darkest tunnels of hardship, mental turmoils leading to helplessness towards the light of hope, understanding, compassion, and self-realization. The poems serve as guideposts, offering readers insights into not only surviving challenges but thriving amidst them. They are a tribute to every individual who has faced life's storms and has emerged stronger.

Dr. Gupta's work also delves into the realms of psychological resilience and the human psyche's intricate dynamics. Her understanding of psychological abuse, its impact, and the path to recovery is profound and enlightening. These poems are more than just reflections; they are tools for healing and empowerment.

As you turn the pages of "The Lotus Life," expect to embark on a transformative journey. In a way, these poems are a mirror reflecting struggles of a common person and a map guiding us towards personal growth and inner peace. It is a privilege to invite you to experience the depth, beauty, and wisdom contained in Dr. Gupta's work.

Contents

1. Smiling Assassins 1
2. Sold 3
3. Murderer 5
4. Naked 7
5. Content 8
6. Silence 10
7. Once More 11
8. Façade 13
9. Perfect 14
10. Shameless 16
11. Intimidating 18
12. Paradise 20
13. Euphoria 23
14. Rainbow 24
15. Golden Hour 25
16. Firefly 26
17. Fear 27
18. Green 29
19. Escape 31
20. Destination 33
21. Extraordinary 34

1. Smiling Assassins

There is a special breed of Humans
Who are adept at carrying a smile.
A smile so enchanting that it pulls
Like a magnet from a mile.

They flock in Friendly Layers,
Lovers, Colleagues, Relatives and Peers.
Cordial, Cheerful, Congenial and Cozy,
Master Manipulators painting everything rozy.

Such are their ways, to win us over
By a fake charm-
Their keen interest-
Is the biggest red alarm.
Never too curious –
but to create a Deadly Harm.

They listen to copy,
Give heed to lobby.
Enablers and flying monkeys
Around them abound.
To keep that void validated
Which in reality is sick and unsound.

Indulging in a massive smear campaigning,
In the game of being supreme and reigning.
Is their favorite Pass time,
Poisonously on the social ladder they climb.
Manipulating the facts with a crafty grin
A narcissist, a toxic abuser within.

Smiling Assasins-
They come and enter without a warning
Become a headache and a lifelong learning
But little are they aware of the power of truth
Which cannot be hushed or muted or silenced
So, the façade wears off and the mask falls down
And a fabricated Hero is hence exposed a clown.

Envy is the mistress of this game of treason
Insecurity grudging without much reason.

2. Sold

"She is for the streets"- echoed He;
After devouring her flesh by the night,
Abandoned her by the sun's first light.
"She is for the treats"-echoed He;
After satisfying his animalistic instinct
Bought her worth with the amount tipped.

Sure she sold and was called a whore
But who was He?
An honorable man with position and status?
Enjoying the perks of privileged social apparatus?

"I can so I do"- proclaimed He;
I am a Man permitted to Sin
You- a mere woman who cannot win
Submit or you shall perish" were his entitled words
Clipped her wings like a caged bird.

Sure she sold and was called a whore
But who was He who sold his soul?
No word, No term to label him?
No taunt, No slander to mock him?

She was for the street because that's what He accord,
Trapped another, alike, in a home where he was the Lord.
Prancing audaciously his corrupt ways,
Did he effortlessly prey night and day.

But who was really sold?
The one selling skin on the street
Or the one buying for his lecherous heat.

3. Murderer

Once there was a girl
As bright as the morning sun;
Full of life, did she live
Cheerful, glad and free;
Until a predator- a fraud did dupe
Her of her glee.

Once there was a girl
As fresh as the blooming lily;
Full of love, did she move
Affectionate, playful and tender;
Until a cheat- a rogue did rob
Her of her dreams.

Once there was a girl
As gushing as a mountain waterfall;
Full of vigor, did she flow
Dynamic, agile and vital;
Until a stooge - a crook did suck
Her of her vigor.
Proudly came riding a horse
To take her in a holy matrimony
Only to register his name on her identity
And mold her into a puppet entity.

Decorating her red to later punish her purple
Was his hidden agenda;
In a garb of a nurturer, he was in real- a Murderer
Accepted and venerated.

Society still called her unholy
For standing up against the abuse;
Her killing was not something new for him
Who thrived on a culture of domination and whim.

He was appreciated by all those known
For thrashing her brutally on the floor
His winning was a metaphor for restoring a culture
Which privileged men for deeds as vulture.

Once there was a girl
As golden as the flames of fire
Burning today on her curated pyre
Slain, killed and murdered to protect a liar.

4. Naked

The day was blazing with the summer heat
Anxiety building in with clocks every beat;
Wearing red lipstick and his favorite perfume
Disgust crept deep into her wounded womb.

She often sat on the window to look outside
Cheerful children playing by the riverside;
The chattering, the chirp of their innocent laughter
Gave her the strength to bear what was doomed thereafter.

Her reverie was shattered when the door creaked
A sound so crass that her soul shrieked;
The echoes of her scream were silently muffled
By stripping her naked and leaving her ruffled.

Breaking and entering without love or compassion
No tenderness, caress or kindling passion;
Every inch of her body and soul was raped
A memory, a scar which she could never escape.
Robbed -physically, mentally, emotionally and spiritually
She was truly left naked brutally;
Underneath the steel grey sheet
By a hand for whom, her heart once beat.

5. Content

"Never Happy, Never Satisfied;
I give her my all and that woman still has gall;
Impossible to understand what this woman still needs?
Ignoring my efforts and my wholesome deeds;
Certainly! Concoct my death and further proceed
In this vicious plan, I would never let her succeed."

"Ain't she lucky to have me as her spouse?
After all I bought her the deluxe sea facing pent house;
She drives the fanciest ride in the town,
And I ensure her girl friends envy her designer gown;
Still she is never Happy, Never Satisfied,
That thankless beauty can never be gratified"

Listening to his rage, she wondered with surprise,
Was she supposed to be content in a union of public eyes?
Content to have a partner giving her ostentatious objects,
And in bargain honesty, loyalty and integrity so conveniently reject?
Content to have a house, a car, money and a gown,
And in bargain keep her worth, self respect and dignity so down?

Her content was love different in need,
His content was material based on greed.
He felt entitled to regulate her and acquire,
and never could fathom what her heart desire.
Like two passengers they travelled on the same road,
But visualized the journey differently while on board.

6. Silence

Was the night singing of dreams
Some inspected and some yet not seen.
I thought of everything passing by
Rolling up in the starry sky
There was a Flash glistening in my eye
Of infidelity getting vivified.

The accord of the bodies was a banal tax
Being paid for urges of the sexual climax
Was this the love she ever want?
A union, a companionship or a mere flaunt
There was a Grief gasping in my sigh
Of adultery seeming typified.

Unsurpassed was the Silence, dancing within them
As It had engulfed all affection and left only condemn
Both looked brazen in their countenance,
One of cheating, the other of endurance.
For night to pass, moonlight is sufficient;
We still light candles as certitude is deficient.

7. Once More

Strangulated Dreams hanging by a rope
Gasping Breath like a hopeless hope
Found her choking as a sorrow soaking
Thrashing her down, Once More.

She was a wilderness wild
God's untainted, uncorrupt, innocent child
Found her trusting a delusionary illusion
Defeating her down, once more.

She lived to live, not to thrive
Undoubting doubt did she survive
Found her weaving a romantic lore
Betraying her down, once more.

She held a vision of the Promised Land
Carving her path with her own hand
Found her captured in an insecure security
Crumbling her down, once more.

Was it her fault to be a giver?
Kind, Genuine and a believer.
"Yes"- they Say, "it is a sin"
To live on Earth and expect every virtue to win.

It is foolish to be expecting expectations
When all people have are mere selfish motivations.
Driven by hidden motives each one operates,
Lust from love very conveniently it separates.

An Unconvinced conviction
Started planting doubts
Concerning her worth, value
And everything that was her All.

It took her a night to cry and let it sink
She wasn't unworthy or too much
Just the right kind with an evolved mind.
Her light shined too bright for those-
used to the blindness;
Her heart beat too pure for those-
used to the adulteration;
She scared their demons which held them captive
Their empty understanding which made them inactive.

Her victory was not for the world to cherish
But an internal battle to not let HER perish.
"Elevate, Fix your crown"- She reminded herself
Broken, Bruised and Bleeding
Yet a GODDESS Rose;
Once More.

8. Façade

A pretense!
Did I just clothe to hide the hideous?
Did I just smile to cover the cries?
Did I just work to survive the stance?
Did I just wake to deny the dying?

A mask- An appearance – A camouflage
Not to mislead but to protect;
The awe- The vulnerability-The Nakedness
Of my soul, my being a whole.

Moonstruck: Mad as a March Hare
A palpable irritability;
Shattering the chains of Chronos
Penetrating the realms of Kiaros.

Urban Filters, choking the idyllic raw;
Suffocating the real, in the name of Law.
 Façade is to guard the élan vital;
Free from the fetters of tellurian titles.

A reality!
Did I just strip to flaunt the flawed?
Did I just weep to reveal the right?
Did I just pause to live the living?
Did I just breathe to believe the becoming?

9. Perfect

A robe is tailor made
For a girl child to wear
Fabric of obedience
Measured with conformity
Stitched with docility
Packaged to be perfect.

A Perfect Daughter
A perfect Wife
A perfect Mother
All in one unified
Never Defiant
Abiding and complaint
A nurturer- A giver
Changing courses like a river

Ever willing to be submissive
Tolerant to transfigure
Approving to alter
Ever ready to be permissive
Of various roles laid in front of her
A self effacing embodiment of perfection.

Popularly accepted- Perfect is draped
In garments easy to maneuver and shape
Wearing them wounds like a soul's rape
A strangulating situation difficult to escape.

I celebrate Imperfect – To Her I invoke
I embrace Imperfect -so I don't choke
I accept Imperfect - to not turn into smoke
I live Imperfect – to be alive and not broke.

10. Shameless

Immodest! Improper! Immoral! Impudent! Declared They.
Defined my breath, Designed my existence;
Instructed me to be self-effacing-
Unboastful! Unassertive! Unobtrusive! Unassured!

Made apprehension, my other Name;
I stooped down, for any chance to Fame.
Alas! Surrendering was a part of the Game;
For which later, I joyfully took the Blame.

Be Quiet- They Said;
Dare not question Us.
Be Silent- They Said;
Dare not resist Us.

Yet I-
Unabashed! & Unafraid! Unbending! & Unashamed!
Refused, Rejected, Renounced, Rebuffed
Any idea that made me less of Me
And Retained-
My One True Self- My Essence
That belonged to no one but Me.
Yes I am a Woman and I have an opinion.
I'm not your coy mistress or your meek angel,
Whose timidness gives you the comfort to lead.

You worship me in temples, sing paeans about me
But only for stories…..
In Real Life my voice intimidates you-
You find it repulsive.
You call me Shameless;
When all I'm trying to be-
Is just "Unapologetically Me!".

11. Intimidating

When you are just a child
Allowed to be boorish and talk wild
Whatever you say is innocent banter –
Encouraged to continue the ceaseless chatter
Pardoned tantrums
Considered harmless and mild.

When you age and have a mind
Expected to be polished and talk refined
Whatever you say is calculated thought-
Discouraged to express the values taught
Accused opinions
Assumed harmful and unkind.

Intimidating is the presence
Preferred is the absence
Of those who refuse to obey
Rules, policies and the unjust way
Labeled arrogant when self assured
Socially unfit and requiring to be cured.

Difficult and Demanding
Threatening and terrorizing
Perhaps! Flattery flatters the flaws
Easily coaxes the ego and applause
The selfdom and the superiority
Interior conflicts of the majority.

Am I intimidating?
Or you intimidated?
The child is pruned
Reduced to be less
Voluntarily comforting the outside
While self assassinating the inside.

12. Paradise

This isn't the story of a conventional sort
A love that is commonly understood and thought.
This is the union of the Sun and the Moon.
One to fire the underlying mystery soon.

It would be farfetched to call it a fairytale;
A cosmic union on a transcendental scale.
Each completing the lack in the other
Celebrating, nurturing and worshipping
One Another.

To love is to stay-
But they, somehow, mastered the art of being away;
Being Away, Perhaps! in distance and time
Yet connected in ways profoundly sublime.

The Sun choose to give away its light,
For the moon to shine bright.
Each required the other more than just a desire,
For their existence, continuance and for being Entire.

If one mastered the art of light,
The other was the champion of the night.
There never was a futile furor,
To label their relationship, so pure.

Both understood the teachings of the Universe,
Where relying on worldly attachment is a curse.
Letting Go! Was their predominant essence,
Rejoicing each other's presence in the simultaneous Absence.

It's inevitable for night to fall after a long day,
When Sun goes down and it's time for Moon to Play.
Both come and go at their own pace,
With assurance that none can each replace.

This story is hence of those two,
Who honored love in all its hue.
Light is acknowledged when there is wisdom of the Dark,
On such as astral journey does Love leave an indelible mark.

Love! They say is a feeling which makes us fall,
They wondered sometimes if that's the falsity of it all.
They never lived romance the easy way,
But wed together even in their distant ways.

Surpassing Conventions and the standard norms,
They rebelled and how a celestial connection could they form.
They loved and yet never complained the distance,
For they automatically believed in each other's persistence.

In Dreams, in visions and in reality,
They merged into one and surrendered to almighty.
A union so rare which feared no Fear,
Of separation, of rejection or society's dishonest layer.
Hence,
The Sun willingly paints the sky inglorious gold,
So Moon mysteriously the night can mold.
It is the rarest of rare phenomena that nature beholds,
Where Day and Night co-exist but never really hands they hold.

13. Euphoria

The timeless joy of running in the meadows,
To listen to the endless laughter through the echoes.
The perennial delight of sipping in the tea,
And relive the sight of romancing she.

She was the epitome of charm and grace,
A luminous aura on that ambrosial face.
She was not the first I had fallen for
But she was the first and the rarest of all.

It felt like a spell that deterred me to propel,
Those pleasures unknown made my heart swell.
Like the pearl underneath an ocean,
She was poetry, a mystery in motion.

Like a shooting star, her presence was fleeting,
Yet her memories were complete and concreting.
Although intangible and out of sight;
She etched an indelible mark in all its might.

The numberless moments with others were numb,
For one single ecstasy, I would willingly, still again succumb.
Those chosen ones who blind drink love
Re-create Paradise and bring the heaven from above.

14. Rainbow

The rain was pouring down,
and sun was shining high;
A radiant rainbow was painted,
on the canvass of the sky.

Violet and Blue and Green and Yellow
The hues smiled from ear to ear,
"Look! a colourful swing in the sky"
"What a splendid sight, Mom, Look there!"

"Why don't you tint your face too, Mom?
Smear it with some red and coral balm;
You will brighten up just like the sky
You needn't hold onto the past happenings and WHY?"

Life is a complex mesh,
Indeed, an entwined puzzlement!
Strangely; both sun and rain are equally vital,
Just as for the sky's anointment.

15. Golden Hour

The sun goes down ready to be set
And the birds fly back to their cozy nest.
Hustle and bustle of the town is at its peak
And the sky is painted crimson with sun's streak.

People return back after yet another tiring day
And recuperate to leave their worries away.
Streets are lit up with artificial club light
And the ambience is set ready for the onset of the night.

Golden Hour reminds that every sun setting
Provides with an opportunity for forgetting
Daily mistakes, failures and woes
And become a diamond with these constant blows.

It is the actual dawn- a second chance to win
Add a new chapter to one's life and a new journey to begin.

16. Firefly

When days are dark and make no sense
When nights are long and look so dense;
A mournful shudder- hopeless and intense
Engulfs my mind- helpless with no defense.

When such occasions become predominant
And there seems no respite;
I often question Providence
If despair is all my Right?

On one such night on an empty stretch
Marching through my Gloom;
A firefly caught my eye-
Amidst the darkness-
Steadily did IT glow and bloom.

I wondered in awe and astonishment
A creature so small, yet so resilient;
Filled the Cimmerian Shade
With sanguine illumination and light,
Perhaps! The Universe responds,
Through such secret simple sights.

In the flicker of a second
That firefly became one with the vastness;
But with it flew away-
My melancholy and my sorrow
And from thence,
Faith became my new friend-
My today and my morrow.

17. Fear

I was once trapped by an inner voice,
An alter ego telling me to fright.
Every new opportunity that came my way
Was dismissed by this usurper;
That deep within my psyche lay.

I held a vision, a golden dream
Unattainable though it seem,
For this false reality reigned supreme
In my mind did it deceitfully scream
That my sense of self is far too extreme.

I sat one day with this terrifying boss
Started that difficult conversation over a drink
Looked daringly into his eyes that bullied me
Questioned authenticity of his overarching authority
And performed a cathartic ritual to let myself get free.

Fear : A misleading feeling that held me back,
Convinced me about everything that I Lack.
Deterred me on my way to glory,
My higher purpose in life's story.

Fear is that which within us resides,
Triumph or Failure thus it decides.
Makes us suffer hypothetical scenarios
Never lets us believe our true potential
Voicing to settle for the bare minimum
But greatness lies on the other side of the horizon
Where Fear becomes our friend and
Metamorphoses into Faith.

18. Green

The warm embrace of the sun's ray
The cool caress of the wave's play
The gentle kiss of the wind's trance
The wild bliss of the earth's dance.
Green is worn by Mother Nature
A creator; A nurturer
None mightier in stature.

But Green is the robe of envy too
Spite, malice, hatred and You
Jealousy in its sinful mischief
Corrupts the mind like a thief.
Human Nature is a motley of emotions
Some virtuous; Some Dark
None so complicated and stark.

Mother's Green paved way for prosperity
While Human's Green gave birth to poverty
One sustaining, growing and satiating all
The other plaguing, killing and speeding the Fall.

I sit in the lap of the infinite presence
And questioningly observe man's self made Green Greed
Hoping for a hopeless answer for my worry
Calling out people to ascend and to hurry.

To Break the Matrix
And Transcend
Act as warriors of the Rainbow
The Golden Race that moves in Grace
Whose language is Love that is selfless
Whose existence is multidimensional
Whose vibration transcends the carnal desires
Whose wisdom merges into the consciousness higher.

To such an Awakening : Open your All
Reclaim the Green and release the Gall.

19. Escape

Raised to believe –
A Happy Place
A Journey of Bliss
Is paved through Pleasure;
I dismayed majorly
Rattled and Knocked down
By Life's Shenanigans.

The constant running after Happiness
Everlasting Pleasure and
Endless dozes of Dopamine;
Made me mad with fury
When life got dull and dreary
I preferred ESCAPE in a hope to cope
That social ethos:
Cemented as a comforting trope.

Comfort is a mistress, a seductress
Weaving an unreal reality
Captivated by her charm
I submitted to an inert inertia
Not willing to rise and explore
And experience what life had to offer more.
I preferred ESCAPE in a hope to cope
That patterned thought:
Entangled and hence my Growth was caught.

To grow is to unlearn
To suffer from the slings and arrows of life.
To experience loss, disappointment, illness, aging
And eventually Die.
There is a choice:
To Run Away or
To Face It and Transmute!

It is only when we go through Fire,
Befriend the Darkness and the sorrow dire;
Consciously Step Up to rise,
Face the difficult reality and become wise;
Doors of miraculous transformation, abundance and blessings unfold;
By this paradigm shift- OUR mental blocks break and a new tale is told.

A journey to bliss is a road strewn with both pleasure and pain.
At Last, when I sat with my inmost demons
Refused to Escape;
Did I, cope, for real
Seeped in a clarity deeper and not vain.

20. Destination

To clear that exam was once a dream,
To crack that interview was a wish supreme.
To own that house was everyday prayer,
To marry that love was the only care.

All 'that' was passionately chased and later replaced
'That' which was once embraced and later displaced
As there was an endless search
For a better option-
A better job, a better place and a better person
A destination addiction -
which exponentially worsened.

21. Extraordinary

My hoggish Friend!
You are so swift, agile and quick
You run a race with a lightening pace
You strive to shape the ordinary, into
Extraordinary;

Yet I see no calm, no joy ; but fear
Insecurity is the cape which you constantly wear.
Why is your desire, not to be an 'Ordinary'
Unrequited?
Perhaps what you attain is contrary.

I see you run and I see you fall,
I see you win and lose it all.
Your eminence, your fortune
Like a flickering wick
Leave your side in a mere click.

Then why?
The haste, the hunger and an insatiable appetite
Why not rejoice?
The ordinary, the normal and the quiet.

Extraordinary!
Beware of her "Elfrin Grot".
Her bewitching charm,
Your acumen might rot.

Don't you think?
Sanity and Rationality,
reside with
Lucidity and Stability.

Vain tiring to conquer the universe,
Achieve it all to make your malady worse;
Instead! Why not celebrate the ordinary joys?
Live, Breathe and not always exert
in your chase for the growth spurt.

Balance the scale, for life is frail
Assimilate in the present, for future is pale.
Attend not to this Extraordinary,
a ravenous dread!
for "Fools rush in where, Angels fear to tread".

www.ingramcontent.com/pod-product-compliance
Lightning Source LLC
LaVergne TN
LVHW061605070526
838199LV00077B/7175